SEASON TO SEASON

A Year in the FOREST

by Christina Mia Gardeski

PEBBLE
a capstone imprint

Pebble Plus is published by Pebble, an imprint of Capstone.
1710 Roe Crest Drive, North Mankato, Minnesota 56003
www.capstonepub.com

Library of Congress Cataloging-in-Publication Data is available on the Library of Congress website.
ISBN 978-1-9771-1289-7 (hardcover)
ISBN 978-1-9771-2005-2 (paperback)
ISBN 978-1-9771-1290-3 (eBook PDF)

Summary: From hibernation to young animals and falling leaves, life in the forest changes from season to season.
Discover why snow is good for trees. Learn what lives and grows in the forest throughout the year. Real-life
photographs follow the seasons and capture the beauty of a year in the forest.

Editorial Credits
Elyse White, designer; Jo Miller, media researcher; Tori Abraham, production specialist

Image Credits
Alamy: New Mindflow, 5; iStockphoto: Alex, 21; Shutterstock: Aleksandr Rakutin, 9, Anastaslia Malinich, 19, irina02,
17, Julia Lav, Cover, (bottom right), Marton Szeles, 13, nampix, 11, Nau Nau, 7, Olga Danylenko, Cover, (top right), 3,
Reimar, 15, S.Borisov, Cover, (bottom left), Simon Bratt, Cover, (top left)

Design Elements
Shutterstock: Alexander Ryabintsev, Minohek

Printed and bound in China.
002493

Note to Parents and Teachers

The Season to Season set supports national science standards related to earth science. This book describes
and illustrates how life in a forest changes with the seasons throughout the year. The images support
early readers in understanding the text. The repetition of words and phrases helps early readers learn
new words. This book also introduces early readers to subject-specific vocabulary words, which are
defined in the Glossary section. Early readers may need assistance to read some words and to use the
Table of Contents, Glossary, Read More, Internet Sites, Critical Thinking Questions, and Index sections of
the book.

All internet sites appearing in back matter were available and accurate when this book was sent to press.

Table of Contents

Spring Is Here!

The sun peeks through the trees.
A new season begins. Spring
is here! Moss grows and buds
dot the trees. The forest turns
green from bottom to top.

Melting snow fills streams and waterfalls. A fawn drinks by its mother's side. People fish in the fresh water. Animals stop hibernating. They look for food.

Hello, Summer!

The seasons change. Days get longer. Hello, summer! Leaves fill the treetops. Shade covers the forest floor. Ferns and wildflowers grow in the soil.

9

Birds sing as bees buzz between flowers. Ladybugs hide under leaves. Visitors set up tents nearby. At night, crickets chirp outside the camp.

Fall Appears!

Soon days grow shorter
and cooler. Fall appears!
The animals are busy.
Squirrels collect seeds and nuts.
They build nests in trees.

Bears eat lots of berries.
Animals grow thick fur.
This will keep them warm all
winter. Colorful leaves fall from
the trees. Winter is coming.

Welcome, Winter!

Snow falls on the quiet forest.

The seasons change again.

Welcome, winter! Snow is good

for the forest. It keeps the soil

and tree roots from freezing.

17

Many animals and insects hibernate. Bears curl up in dens. Ladybugs hide in old logs. Snowshoes leave tracks on the empty trails.

Soon the forest will awaken in spring. The seasons change four times each year. Follow the seasons on a trail in the forest. An adventure might lie ahead!

Glossary

bud—a small growth on a stem that will grow into a leaf or flower

fawn—a young deer that is less than 12 months old

fern—a flowerless, leafy plant that makes spores instead of seeds and can grow on the forest floor

forest floor—the ground of the forest which is covered by a thick, rich layer of soil

hibernate—to rest during the winter; when animals hibernate their body temperature drops and breathing slows

moss—a soft, short plant without flowers that grows on rocks, bark, and damp ground

season—one of the four parts of the year; winter, spring, summer, and fall are seasons

snowshoe—a light wood or metal frame that people wear under their boots to walk on the snow without sinking

soil—the top layer of earth where plants grow

Read More

Gardeski, Christina Mia. *All About Forests*. North Mankato, MN.: Little Pebble, 2018.

Hansen, Grace. *Forest Biome*. Minneapolis: Abdo Kids, 2017.

Waxman, Laura Hamilton. *Life in a Forest*. Minneapolis: Bellwether Media, 2016.

Internet Sites

A Forest Year
https://thekidshouldseethis.com/post/a-forest-year

UC Santa Barbara—Kids Do Ecology: World Biomes
http://kids.nceas.ucsb.edu/biomes/temperateforest.html

Critical Thinking Questions

1. If you wrote a song about the forest, what sound words would you include?

2. Where would be a good spot to camp in a forest? Why?

3. How can we care for the forest?

Index